These poetic visions are a compilation of over 30 years of creative labouring set in this series. Visions 1 is just the beginning. It represents not only my thoughts but, at times, the thoughts or a few words, like sparks from others, that will ignite the fire of a poem within.

I am grateful to Almighty God for upholding me. Likewise, I am thankful for my spiritual family, my natural family and friends, and for the good and bad experiences that encouraged and offered needed help along this journey.

Equally, special thanks to the staff at The Marac Star.tt Centre who afforded me time and their helpful hands to work undisturbed at this facility.

Compiler: Mr. Kwesi Dyer
Graphic Artist and Photographer: Mr. Kwesi Dyer.
Editor: Miss Regina Cozier.
Cover Designer: Mrs. Luanne A. Phillip.
Printery: Graphic Script Printers,
4 Seecharan St. Cane Farm Rd. Tacarigua, T.W.I.

I.S.B.N number: 978-976-8280-45-9

© Anne Saunders 2018.

To: ………………………………………………………………………….

From: ………………………………………………………………………..

Dedicated to: Jonathan Ethan, Jessica Elle, and Jolisa Elise.

THE RAIN FOREST'S BEAUTY

I live in a rain forest,
Oh! How foggy, dark, wet and cold.
Conservation my main interest,
For some weary, sin-sick soul.

What's beautiful about this forest,
Are the varied greens and a little brook.
To capture this magical bliss
Depends on how we see as we look.

The stream trickles every day,
God's tender mercies towards all.
Through the darkness splashes a ray!
Where hope lights over every black wall.

If we focus on the greenery,
We won't see the smog, the gloom, the wet.
Just feel God's tender sympathy,
When life seems one big upset.

All of God's creation,
Is truly a beautiful mystery.
It's our choice, our decision,
To preserve the rain forest's beauty.

THE SUNFLOWER'S SOLITUDE

The sunflower stands alone,
Nourished only by the sun.
It's not in a field at home,
To lean on anyone.

It sways when the storm doth blow;
Not easily ripped apart.
Bowing its head to show...
True meekness of the heart.

Its beauty is no more lessened,
Than that of those in the open field.
As it faces each test, it's brightened...
A radiant beauty to reveal.

Its root system remains unshaken,
Though battered, broken and torn.
To display words unspoken,
For this purpose I was born.

Not faded by life's rugged experience.
Nothing dulls its sunny mood.
It's there by choice, not chance.
The sunflower's solitude.

LOVE

Love doesn't count the cost,
A sinless One felt the pain.
For a sinful world that's lost.
A precious Lamb was slain.

Love doesn't measure the distance,
To save one lost sheep.
To give a sinner a chance,
His soul to secure......keep.

Love doesn't weigh the burden,
The burden of every cross.
To carry the heavy laden,
To light the way of the lost.

Love bears all things,
However painful they be.
Its fountain forever springs,
However costly, heavy, lengthy.

Of such Pure Love I'm unworthy,
My love type can't stand the test.
Lord, pour a little measure within me,
That I could pour out my very best.

FAITH

A little girl held her Father's hand,
Asked him what is faith?
In darkness he had a plan,
To literally demonstrate.

Stand atop of the staircase said he,
While to the bottom he did descend.
Through darkness you can trust me,
I'm your Father...I'm your friend.

Jump he said my child,
It is safe for you to come.
Through the dark she did glide,
Knowing her Dad was at the bottom,

He caught her in his arms,
Trusting, she felt a safety.
A love that heals...calms,
A beacon to the lost and lonely.

It penetrates the darkest night,
Wipes the most sinful slate.
It's an eternal love-light;
Now you know what is faith.

THE TONGUE

Tis a small member's layout
Alike the helm of a ship.
Alike a bit in a horse's mouth,
The tongue that's prone to slip.

Blazing the course of nature,
A world of iniquity.
An unruly, unkind fire
Defiling my whole body.

Birds, serpents, could be tamed
Beasts and creatures of the sea.
No man has ever been named
To tame the tongue in any.

Sends out salt and fresh water
Sends out blessing and cursing,
Sends out sweet and also bitter
An earthly, deathly, fountain.

At the door of my mouth set a watch
Where life and death's power belong.
Where words can have a living touch
Wisdom, please bridle my tongue.

SPOKEN AND UNSPOKEN

No power over the spoken word,
A capturing power I now lack.
It's like freeing a caged bird,
That never will come back.

Alike a sped arrow...it's gone,
Inflicting pain on its flight.
Where it doesn't belong,
A blazing fire to ignite.

When twisted out of control,
Sparks fly for no reason,
The spoken word when told,
Could be a word out of season.

If I did hold my tongue instead,
A friend won't be an enemy.
Regretting discord's ugly head,
Regretting that bird went free.

A secret weapon...my key.
It lifts the heavy burden...load.
It always signs the peace treaty,
Silence...The unspoken word.

DELAY JUDGEMENT

A little girl held out her hands,
With one apple in each.
Judgement delayed stands,
Its vital lesson to teach.

Her mum asked for one of the two,
In a soft and gentle way.
She bit them both seeking a clue,
Disappointing her mum that day.

Judgment did its evil grapples,
As it raced through mum's mind.
When the child bit the apples,
She appeared so selfish...unkind.

A bitten apple she then handed,
Innocently, Happily to her mum,
And said, I just quickly tasted,
To give you the sweeter one.

Do unto others what I will unto me,
A love lesson for every event.
Before passing the death penalty
Let us always delay judgement.

LET ME NOT HEAR AND SEE

Let me not hear and see, the raging billows,
Upon life's stormy sea.
But keep the peace that flows,
Beside the still waters in me.

Let me not hear,
The lion's angry roar.
Stunning, injecting fear.
Shutting faith's precious door.

Let me not see,
The giants of the land.
Only the milk and honey,
Only God's provision.

Let me not hear,
Gossip, rumour, hearsay.
Help me to burden bear,
Than judge weak vessels of clay.

Who is as deaf and as blind,
As a true servant trusting Thee.
Poisonous seeds will distort the mind,
Let me not hear and see.

I TURN THE SWORD

Upon myself I turn the sword,
Rough tissues to cut away.
Things I tend to secretly hoard,
Etched safe in this vessel of clay.

I'm taking my heart to the theater:
Operating on resentment, self pity.
Hoping not to leave a scar,
Cutting no other but me.

Cutting away is painfully harsh,
Of every unwanted growth.
Putting out spiritual trash.
Performing the surgery I loath.

The sword acts as an invisible watch.
My bayonet in close combat, my war.
Things my conscience delights to touch.
That other eyes haven't seen before.

Dear Father, grant me determination,
Your love is not a broken cord.
Teach me to make every incision,
Whenever I turn the sword.

THERE'S A GLITCH IN MY STITCH

I'm making a wedding dress,
Adorned with precious pearls.
But somehow it's a sheer mess,
However I stitch, there are holes.

I tried to repair the glitch,
But to no avail.
Every time I stitch,
I miss the mark on the trail.

The deadline is nearing,
I don't want to miss the date.
But all this repairing,
Is something that I hate.

I call up my Bridegroom
Telling Him of the situation.
He softly answered, I'm coming soon,
To help you at your station.

He came before the wedding,
He saw my mistakes, every glitch.
Now He is here with me preparing,
At the helm of every stitch.

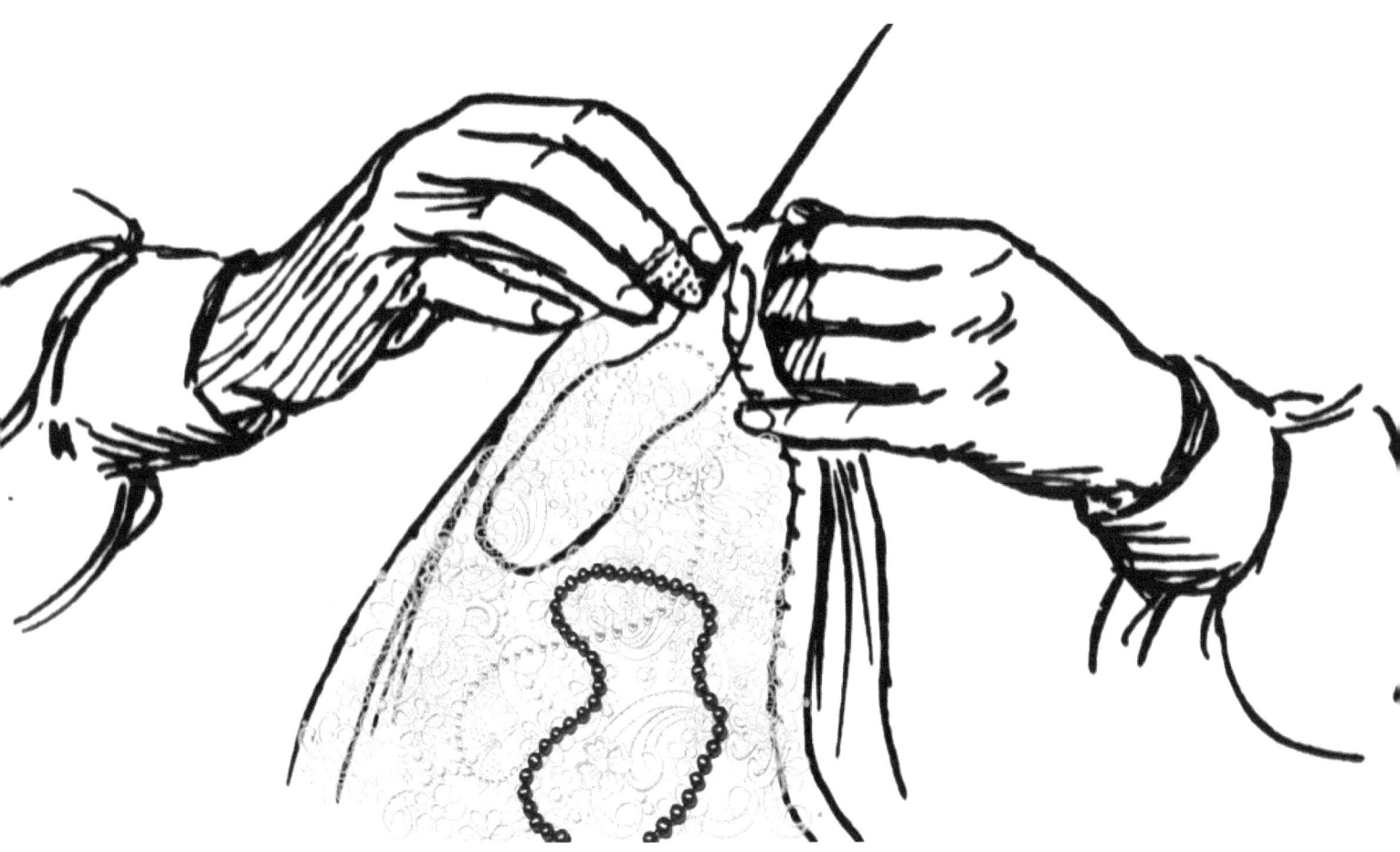

TUNE MY INSTRUMENT

I have an instrument,
Consisting of ten strings.
It sounds a bit different;
To all other musical things.

My main cord the mind, commands,
Two ears, two feet, my tongue.
Two eyes and my two hands
To this instrument they belong.

If my ears and tongue play slack,
My eyes and mind an offbeat too,
Words, thoughts will be off track.
No vision...no focus...no view.

If my hands and feet are loose,
My deeds and steps a black-drop,
I need not make a broken excuse,
I just need to tighten up.

My tuning could be too lax or too tight,
But if my time here is to be well spent,
For all my notes to praise upright,
Lord please tune my instrument.

MY SOCKS DO HAVE A HOLE

My socks do have a hole
And it's hidden in my shoe.
Only Godly eyes could unfold,
What's covered up from you.

My neighbour's dress is torn,
For everyone to see,
I will point at her with scorn
But I can't hide mine from Thee.

Help me to look inside,
And not sit in the judge's seat.
My neighbour could not hide,
But the same error is under my feet.

Don't point at your brother,
With fissures on your heel.
See not the cracks of another;
God sees what we conceal.

Fault finding will always fail true love's test.
It's easier to see my brother's flaws,
But I'm not exempt when undressed,
And let me still treat him as one of yours.

ROWING IN THE WRONG DIRECTION

Oh! Weary soul you are rowing,
Rowing in the wrong direction.
How long will you be travelling,
Towards every strange diversion?

I know you are tired and lonely,
Longing for true love's embrace.
The off course rigours of the sea;
Leaves tracks of tears on your face.

Rowing takes skill and patience,
The vehement gales to meet.
It takes a lot of endurance,
Before your journey is complete.

So if you are rowing, row aright.
The perfect course has a marked path.
Faith a compass a luminous light,
Shines on every sincere heart.

There is a captain who knows a safe course,
We can trust our lifelines to His hands.
When we are in a maze, afraid, lost.
And rowing in the wrong direction.

AGAINST ALL ODDS

Against all odds I run,
No new terrain.
Until the journey's done,
I'll feel that anguish...that pain.

A dead fish down stream will go;
A living one will battle the tide.
Death, no courage...no strength to show.
Life. Thank God His Son died.

Contrary winds must blow our way,
As silver the fiery trial.
To prove in this vessel of clay,
The true meaning of self-denial.

Gold must face the furnace,
To remove the dross...sin's stain.
To lay up heavenly interest,
One must endure agony to gain.

Sometimes, tears do come I cry,
But I cannot go to other gods.
Life to us even though we die,
When we run against all odds.

PATCHES

I'm patching up a little boy,
Whose name is Patches.
Such a lovable toy;
That's just broken matches.

Oh! How I love him dearly,
My Father supplies the glue.
I'll stick him up daily,
Saying, "son, I love you."

Oh! His heart's wounds are so bad,
I kiss him every day.
His sulphur face is so sad,
Tracks of tears and dismay.

When I'm finished with him,
He will light a fire.
He will never see the dust-bin.
Mercy's evident desire.

The kneeling hours are long.
Love fire he catches.
I'll hang in there and be strong,
For my little match boy Patches.

A WOUNDED SOLDIER

I'm just a wounded soldier,
Wounded in the line of duty.
But my brother's wounds are deeper,
Deeper than eyes could see.

Do I pass him by?
Without a word of comfort?
Not caring if he'll die,
Do I make that extra effort?

Do I apply the balm?
Do I carry him to the nearest inn?
Forgetting my painful position,
To go twain with him?

Do I sit back and tend my own will?
My burden is enough says the flesh.
Selfishness is our own standstill.
Selflessness will certainly stretch.

The battle-field will always be there.
The wounds are for everyone.
Lord, teach me how to share and care.
Tis a wounded soldier's song.

STOP, DROP AND ROLL

My soul is on fire,
Im spiraling out of control.
It's consuming my desire,
I must stop, drop and roll.

I must stop the worrying,
What may or may not be.
Because I can't fix anything,
I must stop the anxiety.

I must drop to my knees and pray,
Pray for the abundant rain.
Then await its needed spray.
To soothe my soul's deep pain.

I must roll all my care,
Any time night or day.
Upon one Who's always there,
Upon one Who knows the way.

Then the fire won't singe...burn,
It won't destroy my soul.
Because I'm not left alone,
When I stop, drop and roll.

FORGIVENESS

I take a brother captive,
In my inner prison.
Hoping there he'll live,
For many a varied reason.

With no liberty in sight,
A dim place he'll dwell.
His day is akin to night.
In that prison cell.

His torture...his torment,
Will somehow never cease.
No sun shiny moment,
Until his release.

To solitaire he'll belong,
Alone, dark and cold.
Only known to one,
The possessor of his soul.

When I truly forgive,
When I set at liberty.
Then I'll freely live,
Without that prisoner in me.

HUGGING POWER

Two children had a fight,
A peacemaker I had to be.
I had to set things right,
For them to run along freely.

I told them God is listening,
Only one face had that fear,
No one sided blame shifting,
Only the truth I will hear.

The other face had his version,
Wanting that comfort...pity.
When light came into position,
It was a very different story.

The little boy said it was true,
Admitting he was wrong,
Then this is what he chose to do,
That wasn't very strong.

Now shake hands and say sorry,
He did without a murmur,
Then he did this voluntarily,
He applied his hugging power.

LOVE COMES FULL CIRCLE

I'm just a little troubled child,
In an adoption agency.
My name will come off the file,
When somebody loves me.

I went home with many,
But made no connection.
Then back to the company.
After each rejection.

A couple took me briefly,
On trial into their space.
Into their heart's sanctuary.
Placement closes my case.

True love comes softly,
Comes full circle, to appreciate.
They first loved me dearly,
Loved me in my troubled state.

On my way back to the agency,
I turned to the driver.
Can I call you daddy?
Yes!! was the answer.

AN EXCLUSION ZONE

I need an exclusion zone
In the air, land and sea.
Protecting what is not my own,
Privately entrusted to me.

This zone could get broken
When I lack commitment.
If husks around me has spoken
If engrossed is my time spent.

I must push back the enemy,
My constant temptation...trial.
Keeping the boarders free
With daily self denial.

When foes try to retake
This private territory,
Fasting...prayer I must make.
To say no to the world and me.

Here the spiritual realm is real,
We don't have to fight alone.
Death is life on the battlefield
In this exclusion zone.

FIND A SECRET POCKET

Find a secret pocket,
And hurl yourself inside
The world will see you a misfit,
When you find this place to hide.

You will hear the waves rustle,
The ripples as the stones roll.
You're escaping from the hustle,
As you steal away from this world.

You will hear your own heart beat,
Waves of your own self will.
Your reason must be complete,
Your reason to learn to be still.

You will hear the ocean's sweetness,
A silent effective calm.
Deep under a chorus of quietness,
Amidst the tumult...balm.

Whenever unsettled you feel,
Caught up in the waves above.
Having a need for refresh...zeal,
Find that secret pocket of love.

AMBITION: A DESERT FLOWER

If I had a choice I wouldn't choose,
The desert, the lonely wilderness.
But Your choices Lord, are like chequered hues,
Black and white patches to my own bliss.

Shut out and off from what others enjoy;
Not my will Lord but Thine.
You know what's best for any decoy,
Contentment of spirit will keep me in line.

Just like those succulent desert flowers,
That remain dormant for many seasons,
But with a smattering of rain not showers,
They bloom lavishly it's their reasons.

We can't dictate where we should grow,
In the desert or fertile soil.
Only the best You will bestow,
Help me to bow and willingly toil.

Experiences one can't determine their length.
Dormancy is something I cannot afford.
Please send the drizzles for my strength.
Ambition: A desert flower Lord.

LOVE-SEEDS

The Master plants love-seeds,
Along life's rugged path-way.
They grow among thorns...weeds.
Yet brightens the darkest day.

His dear Son tends the garden,
He waters it daily.
His shed blood gives them pardon;
As He sprinkles them with mercy.

They bloom wherever planted,
Selflessly they shine.
Their love is sure...unlimited...
A sweet fragrance lingers behind.

At the peak of full bloom;
Each one is picked for its beauty.
A life beyond the tomb,
Where naked eyes can't see.

They are carried to a better place,
Through Death's vale, His Son leads.
The Master's table to grace,
Tender, precious, love-seeds.

MY TIME ACCOUNT

My time account is in an hourglass,
I cannot let it wastefully glide.
Very soon it will someday pass,
As life filters to the other side.

At birth this timer is set.
No one knows death's date.
At the end we could either regret
Or trust life's business to faith.

My account closes on this shore.
Times up!! No more calls.
The crossover is forevermore,
When the last grain of sand falls.

It's a timely investment,
With a perpetual life interest.
It could be ruined or well spent,
To everlasting doom or bliss.

God's eyes will see each transaction.
However short or long the amount.
His Hand could guide the transition.
Of our timeless time account.

WHERE NIGHT AND DAY ARE THE SAME

The darkness and the light,
Are both alike to Thee.
Complications, hidden insight.
Lord, to You there is no mystery.

Even the night shall light about me,
Where I feel my sins could hide.
There is nothing Lord, You cannot see;
Both the outer and the inside.

Thou knowest my thoughts, words and deeds,
My down setting, my uprising.
Before I sow the seeds,
You know what I'm thinking.

I wish not to flee from Your presence,
Thankful for Your all seeing eyes.
Where mercy and truth knows no absence,
Molding us to child size.

To You black and white are transparencies.
Save us from eternal shame.
Too late may be our apologies,
Where night and day are the same

THE MASTER REFINER

"When I see My image in the silver,
I know it is refined."
Words of the Refiner,
A precious metal to shine.

To burn away every impurity,
The Smith places it in the centre,
Timing the furnace attentively,
Vigilance of the Master.

The Master Smith is nearest,
Working to perfection.
Working with keen interest;
In all His wisdom.

He will patiently watch, hold and sit,
Recreating this metal at best.
Knowing these hot spots benefits,
The hot spots of each test.

Whether brass, silver or gold,
God's image He'll love to see.
In the fires He'll keep every soul,
Who seeks Him prayerfully.

About the Author

Xerophyte (pronounced Zero-Fit) is ah Trini to de bone, not perfect, with much room for improvement. Just a work in progress who loves Trinidad and visualizes a better place, if only we could take a look in the Master's mirror.

The author envisions too, that by injecting living poetry into our veins, introspection can be induced, thus, healing to rescue our remaining good qualities that we may fully bloom again.